INCREDIBLE ANIMALS!

Eye-opening Photos of Animals in Action

playBac
PUBLISHING
More.Brain.Power

Animals are incredible! While they can be a lot like us, they are pretty different, too!

Taken by photographers who are passionate about nature and animals, these photos capture animals in a whole new way. In the following pages, observe the surprising tenderness of a crocodile, the impressive courtship display of a lovesick frigate bird, the unexpected agility of the penguin, the lively dance of the sifaka lemur, as well as fascinating facts about pelicans, frogfish, hedgehogs, whales, glowworms . . . and much, much more!

Impressive—and sometimes frightening—these photos have been selected for their energy, emotion, and fun. They are an invitation to a fabulous voyage across the land and into the sea, and to amazing discoveries—each more surprising than the last.

Turn the page to begin your trip around the world, and to learn about animals from a whole new point of view.

Hedgehogs like to swim, and they are very good swimmers. But they have difficulty getting out of a pond or river once they've had enough of the water! They must find gently sloping riverbanks to use as exit ramps. Because they can easily become too tired to keep up their hunt for the perfect slope, hedgehogs often use branches and floating bits of wood to help them crawl steadily and safely back to shore.

The crocodile carries her newborn baby between her impressive jaws.

In order to protect her babies from predators, a mother crocodile often carries them between her knife-sharp teeth. A baby crocodile's enemies are numerous, and even include other crocodiles. But if you see a crocodile with her mouth open it doesn't mean a baby is inside. Crocodiles are unable to sweat, so they often keep their jaws open to allow cool air to circulate over the skin in their mouths. A scary way to keep cool!

The leaf-cutter ant can carry a leaf five times heavier than she is!

Certain leaf-cutter ants spend their day harvesting leaves. These leaves are taken back to the ant nest where they are chewed up. The ants in the nest actively cultivate the chewed-up leaves into a fungus, keeping it free of pests and feeding it with more freshly cut plant material. In less than twenty-four hours, the fungus is harvested by other ants and fed to the ant larvae. Yummy!

Male giraffes often fight to see who will rule the group.

While the females stay away with their young, male giraffes brawl for dominance by giving one another blows to the legs and neck. Like horses, they project their two hind legs behind them in order to give violent kicks. These painful blows can sometimes be mortal for smaller animals. Even lions are scared to attack an adult giraffe!

The gazelle can jump over six feet high!

Gazelles are often chased by other wild animals of the savannah, so they must always stay on their guard. As soon as a gazelle notices a predator nearby, it seems to dance in place for a few seconds in order to warn the other gazelles. Then it flees by quickly leaping into the air. The only chance that the gazelle has to escape is by using its incredible speed, which can reach more than forty miles per hour!

This lizard from Australia is the color of a dead leaf!

This very rare little lizard, called the Southern angle-headed dragon, measures only a few inches long. Very distrustful, it becomes invisible in the forest thanks to its being the same color as a dead leaf! If it is seen, it often uses its prickly crest to intimidate enemies. And if that does not work, it quickly runs away. Thanks to its long fingers, this lizard can climb rocks and trees without trouble.

The brown pelican uses its beak, shaped like a pocket, to scoop up fish.

In mid-flight, the brown pelican will dive into a school of fish, beak open and stomach empty! After the catch, it lifts its head and spits out the seawater (but is careful not to accidentally spit out any fish). The pocket of its beak can hold two gallons of water—allowing the pelican to catch up to four pounds of fish a day!

The elephant seal can't do without his friend, a little bird called the cinclode.

While this arctic bird is five thousand times smaller than the elephant seal, both depend on each other. The cinclode fearlessly approaches the colossal elephant seal because he knows that the little parasites living in the folds of the seal's skin are good eating, and the elephant seal can't wait to get rid of the scratchy things! Sometimes the elephant seal even falls asleep while the cinclode nibbles away.

These herds of gnu travel in groups of many millions.

Each springtime, millions of gnu, also called wildebeests, migrate thousands of miles from East Africa toward the North in search of water and fresh pastures. Along the way, these immense herds have to cross rivers inhabited by predatory crocodiles. Therefore, during these long migrations, the gnu have to race through the water in an effort to avoid being devoured by these ravenous reptiles.

The great white egret is capable of fighting in midair!

This very elegant white bird can be hostile with his flying companions. The fights are frequent and often violent, with pursuits, blows, and shrieks. But calm quickly returns, and the egrets make peace and go back to fishing along swamps and rivers. Currently a protected species, the egret was once hunted for its magnificent white feathers, which were in great demand by hatmakers.

with his fur thick as a down jacket, the Japanese macaque is never cold!

Thanks to his thick fur, the Japanese macaque, also known as the snow monkey, is capable of enduring snow and temperatures that can plummet to -4 degrees Fahrenheit. If he does start to feel the chill, the Japanese macaque lounges in hot springs all day long!

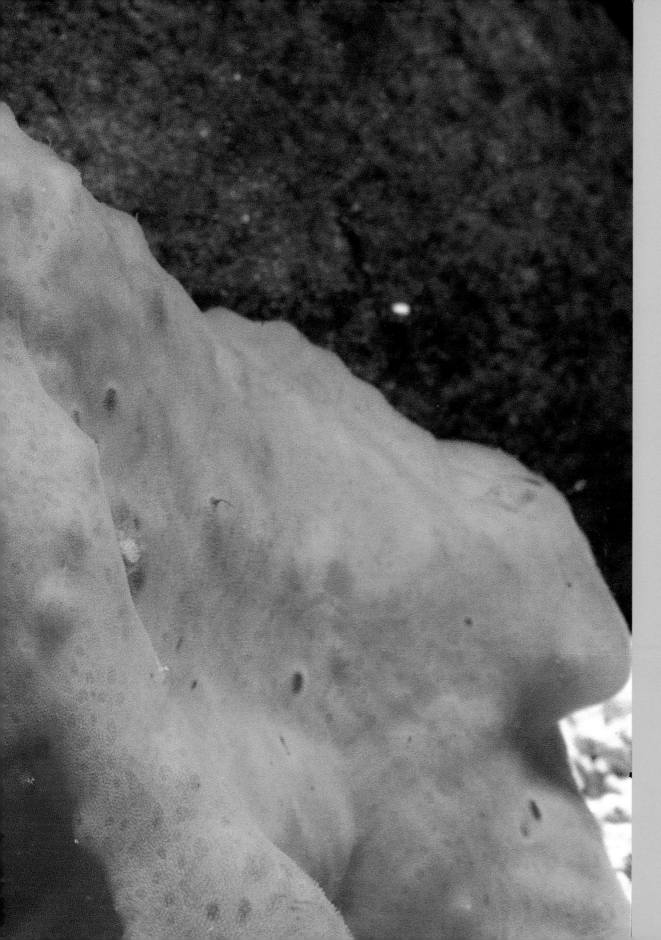

In order to hunt successfully, the frogfish disguises itself.

Whether it's on the sand or in the middle of rocks, the frogfish of the Caribbean can change its shape and color in order to blend in with the background. But while most animals use camouflage to conceal themselves from predators, the frogfish uses it to hunt. An unsuspecting fish might swim toward what it thinks is a rock—only to find that it's the frogfish's dinner! And because it has an enormous stomach, the frogfish can swallow prey as big as itself!

To find a mate, the male weaverbird builds the most beautiful nest possible.

In half a day, the male weaverbird can build a nest with over three hundred feet of grass and small branches. When he has finished the nest he begins to sing and dance, hoping a female weaverbird will enter. Strangely enough, as soon as she is inside he immediately begins another nest in order to attract another mate!

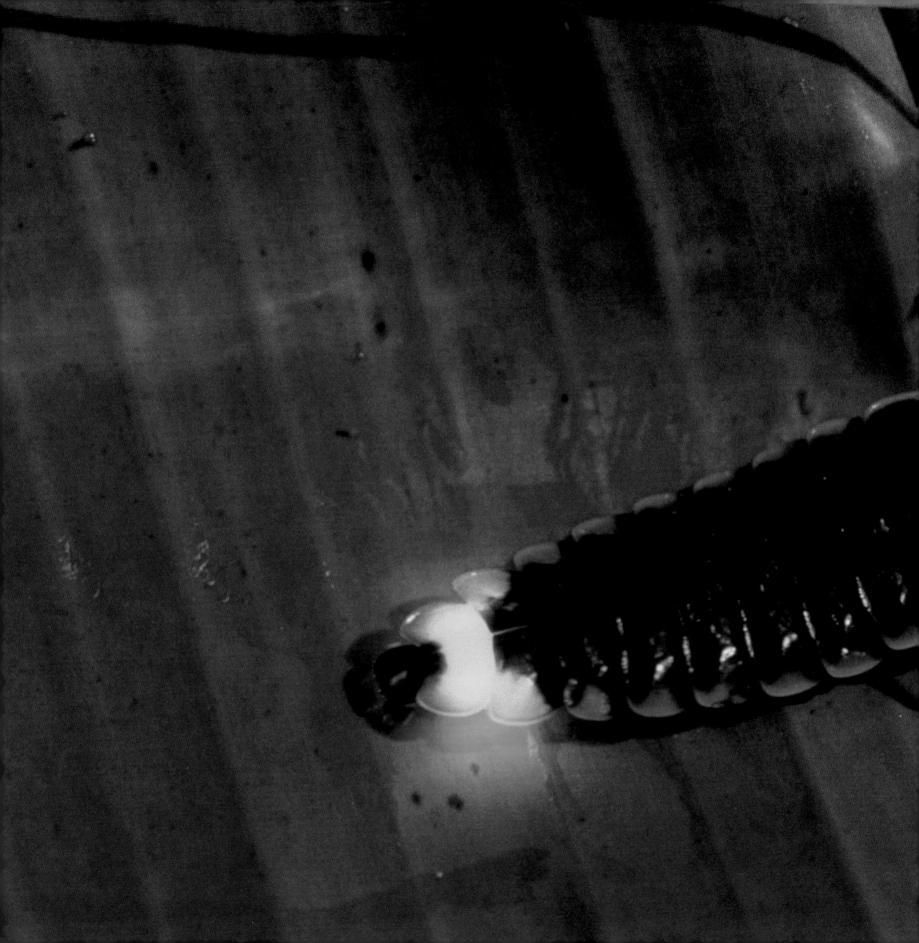

The female glowworm really glows!

Perched on a blade of grass, female glowworms attract males with a glowing light that they emit from their lower stomachs. Male glowworms recognize the rhythm and the color of the lights and move toward the females. But the female doesn't just use her light whenever she wants: She only blinks if a male of her species is nearby!

Believe it or not, the frill-necked lizard is very shy!

Despite his frightening appearance, this Australian lizard is always nervous when he goes for a walk. In order to make his enemies think he is big and dangerous, he flares the pointed scales on his back and throat like an umbrella. Then he hisses menacingly and whips his tail into the air. And if all that doesn't work, he simply runs away!

The Javanese flying squirrel is capable of soaring from tree to tree!

With his hind legs and front legs connected by a sort of "hairy cape," the flying squirrel, which sees in the dark, can glide in the air after jumping from trees. As soon as he leaps, he extends his "wings" of skin in order to glide as long as possible. While in midair, he steers by using his tail like a rudder. And he uses his claws to grab branches for a smooth landing.

orangutans' arms are longer than their legs.

The orangutans of Asia are the biggest and most solitary monkeys that live in trees. The mother orangutan hangs onto the tree limbs while her baby clings to her long red hair. In order to move securely from branch to branch, she uses all four of her limbs for more security. And in order to rest, she makes a comfortable nest made of branches and leaves.

camels know how to swim!

Camels are famous for their ability to go for long periods without water. In fact, they can live without water for more than eight days. But as soon as they find a lake or river, they can drink fifty gallons of water in a few minutes to "fill up." Sometimes they even like to take a refreshing swim!

The sloth uses his long claws to cling to trees.

Hidden in the heart of tropical forests, the three-toed sloth peacefully chews leaves, shoots, and fruits. When he is done eating, he curls up to sleep for about seventeen hours each day! The sloth doesn't like to move too much—he prefers to move slowly from tree to tree using his long, pointed claws. He only descends to the ground once every ten days in order to dig a hole and deposit his droppings.

The little wild boar piglet is no bigger than a rabbit!

After the birth of the little piglet, the mother sow spends three weeks alone with him before rejoining her group. The baby piglet has a light brown coat with parallel stripes from head to tail. At about four to five months, his fur turns red until the following year when his coat darkens. But at one year, the young males leave the group and live alone. Fully grown male boars often weigh over four hundred pounds!

The osprey can catch fish weighing 4½ pounds!

When the osprey, also called the fish hawk, spots a fish swimming near the surface of the water, it plunges its talons into the fish and snatches it out of the water. Then he carries the captured fish away, always placing the fish's head in the direction of the flight to make flying easier. However, the osprey's talons are *so* good that it can have trouble releasing the fish. And, if the fish is too heavy, the osprey can be dragged back into the water and drown!

Marine iguanas must warm themselves up after their long, cold swims.

The marine iguanas of the Galápagos go deep into the ocean (up to sixty-five feet) to gather and eat cold seaweed. To warm themselves up, they stay in the sun for hours, clinging to rocks with their long claws. Throughout the day, the iguanas change position to face the sun. And, if they get too hot, they raise up on their front legs so that cool air can circulate under their bellies!

The sea otter can eat while floating on his back!

A hungry sea otter catches sea urchins, cuttlefish, and small crabs. To eat, he floats on his back while holding a rock on his belly. The sea otter uses the rock as a tool to break the spines of the urchins or the shells of the shellfish. The otter is such a greedy eater that his teeth can turn purple from eating so many sea urchins!

The walrus's tusks never stop growing!

The two upper canine teeth of the walrus measure close to three feet! The walrus uses these tusks as weapons against killer whales and polar bears, as hooks to climb up on ice floes, and as a way to drag himself along the ice. Inuit people have long hunted walruses for food, or to make weapons, tools, and sculptures from the ivory of their tusks.

Hippopotamuses fight fiercely to defend their territory.

The big canine teeth of the hippopotamus command respect. Male hippopotamuses divide up territories with well-defined boundaries on land and sea. In order to identify their own space, they scatter their droppings and urine. And, if another male dares to cross the line, the owner of the place violently attacks him! Hippopotamuses are so tough, that in order to defend their calves they will not hesitate to fight lions or crocodiles!

The humpback whale can leap out of the water one hundred times a day!

The humpback whale swims from great depths in the sea toward the surface—bursting out of the water before falling back on his side, back, or belly. These leaps serve as much to show off his strength to the other whales as to relieve him of parasites that can get stuck to his back (annoying *and* problematic for swimming). When the humpback falls back into the water, the shock is so violent that the splash is visible from several yards away!

called the strawberry poison dart frog, the *Dendrobates* is no bigger than a thumb!

Because it has tiny adhesive disks under each of its toes, the miniscule poison dart frog of Costa Rica climbs tall palm trees without a problem. Red, blue, brown, or green according to the region it lives in, the poison dart frog is in great demand by native tribes. They use its poison to make deadly blowgun darts that they use for hunting!

55

The male tropical walking stick is as red as a tomato!

While a female walking stick has orange and yellow stripes, the male is entirely red. If a predator takes too much interest in him, the walking stick has numerous weapons at his disposal. He can shoot out irritating liquids, stay still in order to play dead, or discharge unbearable odors. And if all else fails and he is caught, he can choose to release one of his legs in order to escape!

The ringneck snake always swallows its prey alive!

The ringneck snake likes to swim in rivers, ponds, or swamps. It can even dive and stay underwater for fifteen minutes in order to catch a frog or fish. Once it catches something, it brings it back onto land in order to have a leisurely meal. And because the ringneck snake doesn't have any venom, it eats its prey without even killing it first. Amazingly, it's possible for it to regurgitate a still-living toad an hour after having swallowed it!

The Galápagos tortoise is the largest in the world.

Because its shell is slightly raised toward the front, the Galápagos tortoise can look for food by using its neck like a periscope. Giant female tortoises can weigh up to 325 pounds and males can weigh up to 550 pounds! However, because it is so heavy, if the tortoise accidentally gets turned upside down on its back, it is almost impossible for it to get back on its feet again all by itself.

Ladybugs gather by the hundreds to sleep.

In the summertime, ladybugs fly as a colony toward cooler places. When it's autumn again, they take shelter and get ready for hibernation by piling up under tree bark or rocks. Attached to leaves by using their little hooked feet, they can sleep peacefully through the winter. And because their red color frightens predators so much, they don't have to worry about being attacked while they sleep!

mother bear is very strict with her cub!

Among bears, education is entirely the responsibility of the mother. However, her methods are not very gentle! When the bear cub doesn't obey, the mother bear roars and growls right in front of the cub's little head. If that's not enough, she doesn't hesitate to slap him with her paw. And, in order to teach him how to climb trees, she chases him to the bottom of the tree trunk and frightens him into climbing . . . and then calmly waits below for the cub to decide to climb down.

65

The kudu antelope has little chance of escaping a hungry lioness.

If the kudu doesn't have enough of a head start, it is easily caught by the lioness. Even at the height of the kudu's strength and speed, it is not fast enough to outrun the lioness. The kudu's only hope is leaping over terrain that their predators may have a hard time getting around. In one jump, kudu can easily jump over six feet!

The basilisk can run on water!

When he needs to make a quick getaway, this lizard from South America gets up on his hind feet and runs for it! The basilisk spreads out his toes to prevent himself from sinking in the water. He also knows how to swim and dive, and can stay underwater for close to an hour—all in order to escape his predators. According to legend, the basilisk is a combination of a rooster and a snake!

Some elephants can swim for several hours at a stretch.

Among land animals, the Asian elephant is one of the better swimmers. Certain elephants can even swim from one island to another. They hold their trunks above the water to breathe—like a snorkel! Alone or in a herd, the elephant can cross several miles of water each day. Fearlessly, elephants will jump into the sea without worrying about the depth.

Leaf grasshopper: the king of camouflage!

In order to be fully protected, this grasshopper from Amazonia has wings that perfectly imitate tree leaves. The resemblance is an exact match of color, spots, and even the little veins! This skillful camouflage allows the insect to fade into the forest and escape the notice of its enemies. But when its predators *do* approach, the poser grasshopper must stay perfectly still!

The sperm whale's head weighs as much as three elephants!

The sperm whale is the largest marine mammal with teeth. It weighs a ton at birth, and thanks to the fifty gallons of mother's milk it drinks per day, it doubles its weight in a week! The sperm whale is also a champion diver: It can descend two miles into the ocean and swim for two hours without breathing!

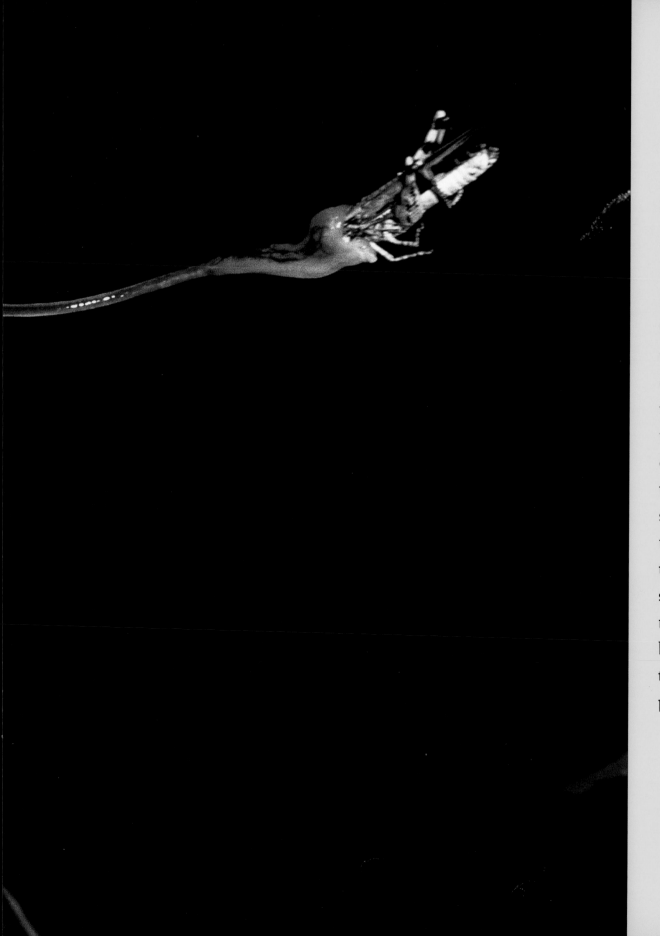

The tongue of the chameleon is as long as its body!

The chameleon has three unique characteristics: It can change color according to its surroundings, its eyes move independently of each other, and it uses its tongue to hunt. When an insect passes nearby, the chameleon darts out its tongue and immediately snaps it back into his mouth. It's been calculated that the chameleon's tongue shoots out of its mouth at more than twenty-six body lengths per second—that's the equivalent of 13.4 miles per hour!

The male frigate bird inflates when he is in love!

During the mating season, the male frigate bird has a very peculiar technique to attract females: He inflates the big pocket of red skin under his beak like a balloon. Then, very excitedly, he shrieks while turning toward the female and beating his wings. She chooses the most inflated male and seizes his beak with hers.

Red-eyed tree frogs are also called monkey frogs.

Hidden under the leaves during the day, red-eyed tree frogs travel at night like monkeys, swinging along branches and vines. When they rest, they keep their eyes closed. But if they are attacked, they quickly open their eyes in order to surprise their aggressor. And while his ememy is temporarily surprised, the red-eyed tree frog flees with a bound, all the while sprinkling the contents of his bladder!

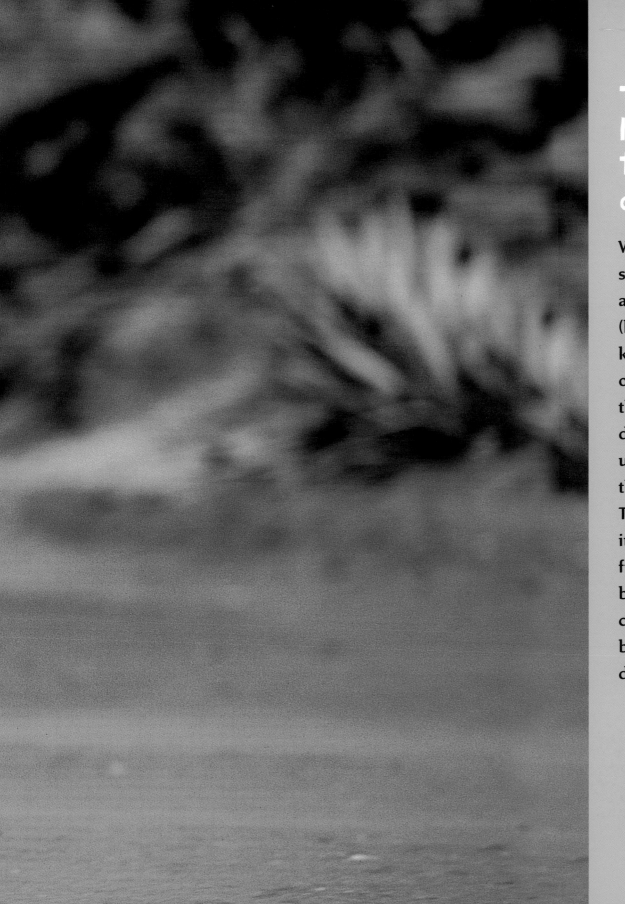

The sifaka lemur always travels by dancing!

When moving forward, the sifaka of Madagascar does a two-legged sideways hop (like a dance step) while keeping its arms spread in order to stay balanced. But these lemurs do not just dance, they can also jump up to twenty-five feet with their powerful hind legs. The jumps are so high that it looks like they are flying from tree to tree. A sifaka's babies, which the mother carries on her back, had better keep a tight hold during each jump!

Tiger cubs are cats that adore swimming!

Tiger cubs can cross great rivers with ease. They are excellent swimmers who jump and play in the water before taking a long nap that can last up to twelve hours. When they grow up, they will even be capable of swimming for six miles! Tigers normally eat red meat, but when they are in the water they will eat frogs or fish.

The penguin shoots out of the water like a rocket!

The emperor penguin is a very unusual bird: He is incapable of flying but knows how to swim very well! Using his wings as fins, he dives into the ocean and can stay underwater for up to thirty minutes. But, if startled, he swims back up to the surface as quickly as possible—propelling himself into the air with a bound that can reach six feet in height!

The polar bear makes his pillow out of blocks of snow.

In the winter, male polar bears hunt seals on the ice floes, while females stay in the shelter of their den with the baby cubs. When the male polar bears get tired, they stretch out on fresh snow and sleep for a few hours. Thanks to their heavy winter coat, composed of a blanket of thick hair and layers of fat under the skin, polar bears are perfectly protected from the cold. Underneath their white winter fur coat, polar bears actually have black skin!

Even when he seems to be asleep, the jaguar is always ready to pounce.

In order to rest, the jaguar stretches out along a branch and lets one of his front paws dangle. But he is a light sleeper. When prey passes below, he quickly leaps into action. Similarly, the jaguar fishes by laying on a branch and lazily striking the water below with his tail. Fish who are curious about the commotion and come up to the surface are soon victims of a swipe of the jaguar's claws!

The leader of the kangaroos always travels with his friends!

During the day, kangaroos rest in the shade of trees, but at night they leave to look for food. To move, they hop on their two hind legs and can leap up to thirty feet in one jump. When they run, their tails don't stay on the ground, but are used for balance and support as they reach speeds of up to thirty miles per hour!

Index

Special Thanks to:

Christopher Hardin, Jennifer Vetter, Cheryl Weisman, L. Maj, L. Bouton, B. Legendre, C. Boulud, John Candell, and Paula Manzanero

Photography Credits

BIOS
6–7: D. Heuclin. 8–9: M. et C. Denis-Hout. 16–17: F. Bruemmer/P. Arnold. 20–21: C. Sams/P. Arnold. 28–29: J. Sierra/OSF. 30–31: A. Mafart-Renodier. 32–33: A. Compost. 42–43: G. Schulz. 52–53: Klein/Hubert. 54–55: Gayo. 60–61: R. Cavignaux. 62–63: F. Bruemmer. 66–67: M. Harvey. 72–73: L.-C. Marigo. 74–75: H. Hall/OSF. 80–81: A. Odum/P. Arnold. 82–83: M. Harvey/Fotonatura. 88–89: T. Mangelsen/P. Arnold. 90–91: R. Cavignaux.
COLIBRI
24–25: C. Baranger. 34–35: A.-M. Loubsens. 56–57 and 78–79: J.-L. Paumard.
JACANA
36–37: MC Hugh/PHR. 38–39: N. Wu. 50–51: A. Shah. 84–85: Photo Researchers.
PHO.N.E.
18–19: Ferrero/Labat. 22–23: J.-P. Ferrero. 46–47: F. Gohier. 48–49: R. Valter. 58–59: Hellio/Van Ingen.
HOAQUI
70–71: P. Bourseiller.
STOCK IMAGE
10–11, 40–41, and 64–65: Stock Image Premium Stock.
SUNSET
4–5: Brake. 12–13: Photo German. 14–15: Animals Animals. 26–27, 44–45, and 92–93: G. Lacz. 68–69: Photo NHPA. 76–77: A. et J. Visage. 86–87: Reinhard.

ISBN-13: 978-1-60214-059-2

Play Bac Publishing USA, Inc.
225 Varick Street
New York, NY 10014-4381

infospbusa@playbac.fr
Contact number : +12126147725

Printed in Singapore

Distributed by Black Dog & Leventhal Publishers, Inc.
151 West 19th Street
New York, NY 10011

First Printing, October 2008

April/2009